Ra

First published in Great Britain in 2006
by Hodder Children's Books
Text © Jenny Alexander 2006
Illustrations © Jennifer Graham 2006
Design by Andrew Summers
Cover design: Hodder Children's Books

1

A catalogue record for this book is available from the British Library

ISBN-10: 0340931272
ISBN-13: 9780340931271

Printed by Bookmarque Ltd, Croydon, Surrey

The paper and board used in this paperback by Hodder Children's
Books are natural recyclable products made from wood grown in
sustainable forests. The manufacturing processes conform to the
environmental regulations of the country of origin.

Hodder Children's Books
a division of Hachette Children's Books
338 Euston Road
London NW1 3BH

Rabbit talk

Jenny Alexander

A division of Hachette Children's Books

Rabbits can live happily indoors or out-of-doors but wherever your rabbit is going to live he will need a safe space where you can leave him on his own - say a run, or a room with all the electrical wires covered. When you're watching him, you can let him have the run of the house, or the garden so long as you've got good fences.

Compared to your rabbit, you are **huge**. Imagine a giant wanted to pick you up - you would be quaking in your boots! When your rabbit first arrives she will be scared so don't just grab her. Sit quietly nearby and give her time to pluck up the courage to come and say hello to you.

Some people say you should pick a rabbit up by the ears. I wonder how they would like it if someone did that to them! Pick your rabbit up slowly and gently, placing one hand on his forehead first to calm him and putting the other under his bottom to support his weight.

Shh ... Your rabbit doesn't like loud noises. Always talk to her in a quiet voice. She won't understand all the words you say but she will soon learn to recognise her name if you use it every time you feed her or pick her up.

I'm sorry - but you're going to find this out sooner or later ... Your rabbit eats his poos! Not the hard little round ones he leaves lying around, but soft squishy ones he eats as they come out. This is because he doesn't get all of the goodness out of his food in one go - he has to eat it twice. Don't try to stop him, or he won't get all the nourishment he needs.

Wheee ... she's off! Sometimes your rabbit will suddenly go on a mad dash around the garden or sitting room, just because she feels like it. She might do several high jumps as she goes, twisting round in midair to change direction. Stand clear and enjoy the fun!

Make a burrow for your bunny out of a cardboard box. Cut a hole in the side just big enough for him to squeeze through - he'll nibble away the edges to make it bigger if he wants to. Stick several boxes together to make it even more interesting for him.

Find out your rabbit's favourite treat.
She might like a little scrap of bread
or the corner of a plain cracker. She
could have a piece of apple or banana.
But remember she's much smaller
than you, so her eat treats shouldn't
be bigger than this ...

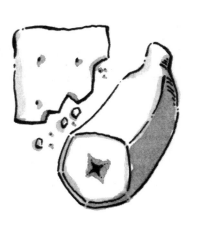

When your rabbit grinds his teeth it's like a cat purring. He'll grind his teeth slowly when he's feeling relaxed and happy. When he's excited he'll grind them really fast and make his whiskers wiggle. Try grinding your teeth softly when you pick him up. See if he replies.

Hmm … I wonder what's in the paper today. Your rabbit will probably devour all the news stories if your dad leaves the paper lying round. At the very least, she'll tear it into shreds with her teeth or try to dig a hole in it. So give her yesterday's paper to play with - and make sure you tidy up after she's finished with it!

Rabbits are liveliest in the early morning and when it's just getting dark. Your rabbit will be at his calmest in the middle of the day so this is the best time for grooming him, especially if he's a bit nervous. Be gentle and use a soft brush. If you're lucky, your rabbit may lick your hand - that's him grooming you.

Watch out for wires! Your rabbit will nibble almost anything, especially wires from your TV or telephone. Some people say that's because rabbits think they look like roots - and when it comes to burrow-digging, roots get in the way. Nibbled wires are dangerous for you and your rabbit so cover them or make sure he stays away.

Why does your rabbit sometimes bob her head up and down? No, she isn't madly agreeing with you, she's trying to get something in focus that she can't see very clearly. Rabbits can't see very far in the distance.

Chocolate and crisps might be yummy for you but they're really, really bad for your rabbit. Never give her anything even slightly sweet, salty or fatty to eat because she'll probably get an upset tummy - and you definitely don't want to have to clean up after a rabbit with the runs.

Sometimes your rabbit might nudge your hand and try to put his head under it. He's saying 'You're the boss' and 'Look after me, please'. Be careful because he may also try to slide his head under your foot when you're sitting down, so check before you stand up again.

What could be better than a new toy? Your rabbit will love cats' toys from the pet shop or a carrot on a piece of string, but don't be disappointed if she doesn't seem too keen at first. Rabbits are nervous of new things, and she'll probably creep up to it very slowly. Let her take her time.

Bang! Your rabbit will stamp both his back feet really hard on the ground if he's alarmed. Maybe he's sniffed something frightening, like next door's dog, or maybe he's angry because he thinks you're going to pick him up and he's not feeling sociable. Stamping is a warning to other rabbits - and to you. Back off!

Sometimes your rabbit might hop away from you with a sharp flick of her back feet and then do a full body shudder as if to say, 'Yuk!'. Think about what you might have done to annoy her, such as picking her up when she didn't feel like it or offering her something to eat that she didn't like - and don't do it again!

Most of the time all your rabbit can see of you is your feet, or your face when you bend down to pick him up. Lie down on the ground and let your rabbit explore you. He will sniff every inch of your legs and arms and even your face - watch out for his tickly whiskers!

Lying down in clean, fresh hay makes your rabbit smell gorgeous like a summer meadow. Pick her up and give her a sniff! Close your eyes and imagine you're in a field full of wild grasses and flowers, just you and your rabbit playing in the sun.

If your rabbit flops over on his side and looks as if he's died, don't worry. He's just feeling happy and relaxed. As soon as you go near him he will sit up. Rabbits don't sleep deeply because in the wild they have to always be on the look-out for bigger animals who might want to eat them.

Share a carrot with your rabbit. Peel
and wash it first, then snap it in half.
Hold one half out for your rabbit to
nibble and eat the other half yourself.
Carrots are really good for rabbits -
and they're really good for you too!

Freeze! When your rabbit is frightened he will crouch down, trying to make himself as small as possible, with his ears flattened against his head. But he will keep his eyes wide open, ready to run if things get really dangerous.

It's a little-known fact that rabbits sulk. If your rabbit gets annoyed with you, she'll turn her back on you and ignore you. But she'll soon forget that she's fed up and stop sulking because rabbits can't remember anything for very long.

Don't let your rabbit get lonely. Remember that wild rabbits live in warrens with hundreds of other rabbits and they don't like being all on their own. Even if your rabbit doesn't want to be held all the time, he will like to have you nearby.

There is nothing in the whole wide world that looks as sweet as your rabbit when she's having a wash! First she will lick her front paws and rub them all over her face and whiskers. Then she will wash her lovely long ears, pulling them down between her damp paws. Time for a photo!

Have you ever heard people call lettuce 'rabbit food'? It's odd because most rabbits don't even like lettuce - it can make them feel sick. Instead of lettuce, give your rabbit a handful of grass or dandelion leaves, or for a special treat, a nice little bunch of parsley.

Don't worry if your rabbit's ears seem really hot. That's because rabbits don't pant like dogs or sweat like horses - they cool down by letting the heat out through their ears. In hot countries, rabbits' ears grow longer so they can let more heat out!

When your rabbit rubs her chin gently on something she is saying 'This is mine!'. Every new object you put into her run will be examined and chinned. She will mark anything new that comes into her territory - from time to time she may even try to chin you.

Rabbits prefer to be picked up from above. If you get down to his level and try to look him in the eye as you're picking him up he could feel threatened and nip you on the nose.

Here are three things that will almost
certainly annoy your rabbit, so avoid
doing them -

1. Picking her up when she's eating or
having a poo
2. Trying to tickle her tummy
3. Disturbing her when she's having
a wash

When you talk to your rabbit she will turn one ear towards you while she keeps the other one on the listen-out for other noises. Get your mum to start talking from the other side of the room, and see how your rabbit directs one ear at each of you.

What is the busiest part of your rabbit? Her nose! It's always twitching, picking up interesting smells. Sometimes she will sit right up on her back feet and stick her nose in the air if there's a particularly interesting smell wafting her way.

Your rabbit needs a little dark den
where he can go to be on his own, like
a burrow in the wild. When he is in his
sleeping quarters don't disturb him.
He'll soon come out to see what's
going on if he hears you nearby.

How does it feel to be like your rabbit? Crouch down in a corner. Put your head up and sniff the air. Do some bunny hops across the room. Can you be as quiet as she is on her soft furry feet?

Your rabbit has three favourite
resting positions -

1. Lying on his side
2. On his tummy with his back feet
   stretched out behind him
3. Sitting with his legs tucked
   underneath him

Try them out for yourself. Which
one feels most restful to you?

Don't try to hold your rabbit on her
back like a baby. She may seem to like
it because she will lie very still, but
that's because she's frightened, not
happy. Being scared could make her
aggressive and she might try to scratch
or bite you as you put her down.

Does it seem like sometimes your rabbit can't see something that's right in front of his nose? That's because he really can't. Having his eyes on the sides of his head means he can see all around him but he's got a blind spot right in front.

If your rabbit is in danger or she's chewing up your mum's favourite plant, clap your hands. The sudden noise will stop her in her tracks. However, she'll have forgotten your warning in no time, so unless you want to spend all day clapping, just move the plant somewhere out of her reach.

When you are holding your rabbit,
be careful he doesn't jump out of
your arms. If he's very lively, it
might be better to sit on the floor to
hold him. Rabbits can hurt their
backs if they try to jump from too
high above the ground.

You can train your rabbit to sit up and beg. Offer her a treat and let her eat it off your hand. Then offer a second one, holding it a little above her head so she has to reach up. The third time, lift the treat a little higher and she'll go up on to her hind legs. Easy peasy!

Your rabbit is one hundred per cent covered in fur - even the soles of his feet. His fur is incredibly soft - especially the little patch under the back of his ears. The white bit under his tail is called the scut. If he's hopping away from danger it acts as a warning signal to other rabbits.

What sounds can your rabbit make? When he's excited he might make little grunting noises, when he's contented he'll grind his teeth and he might huff a bit when he's hot. Rabbits are very quiet pets although they are capable of letting out a loud scream if they're in great pain or really, really frightened.

If your rabbit gets fed up with being held he may start to wriggle and flick his ears once sharply. If you don't let him go, he may try to eat you. Most rabbits only bite if you ignore what they want even though they've made their wishes very clear.

Your rabbit's teeth grow all the time and that's one reason why she's always chewing - she has to keep grinding them down to stop them getting too long. You can help by putting a piece of wood in her run. She'd especially love a bit of branch from a fruit tree.

Rabbits love to dig. Your rabbit will try to dig anywhere he can - in a sand pit, a flower bed or even the corner of the new carpet on your bedroom floor. If he's digging in the garden don't let him get too deep or you might end up having to go next door to ask for your rabbit back!

If your rabbit lives indoors, she'll like to have a bit of time outside each day in the summer but don't let her go out in cold weather or she could catch a chill. If she lives outside, don't bring her indoors to play in the winter or she could catch a cold when she goes back outside.

Ouch! Your rabbit might nip you sometimes, but never ever ever hit him - he won't understand. Try to work out what you did to annoy him instead, and let him teach you how he wants to be handled. Biting is the only way he can tell you, 'Stop doing that!' or 'Don't do that again!'.

Most rabbits are fussy eaters. Your rabbit will probably eat all her favourite bits and leave the rest. See if you can get her to eat the boring bits from your hand. If she's hungry but she doesn't fancy what's left she'll probably pick the bowl up in her teeth and tip it over.

From time to time, your rabbit will moult. Give her a good brush to collect up all the fur that's falling out before you try to cuddle her or else you'll get hair up your nose and all over your sweater.

Rabbits are shy, nervous little animals and it can take a lot of time and gentle care to get their trust. But as your rabbit gets to know you he will gradually feel more confident. Then he'll be up for fun and cuddles, and he'll be your friend for life.